THE SECRETS O...

Fasting is a safe, natural way... ...ed
wastes and teaching it to... ...or
describes the whole fastin... ...al
eating.

THE SECRETS OF SUCCESSFUL FASTING

by

Dr HELLMUT LÜTZNER

Translated from the German by
Linda Sonntag

THORSONS PUBLISHERS LIMITED
Wellingborough, Northamptonshire

First published in Germany as
Wie neugeboren durch fasten

© 1976 Gräfe und Unzer GmbH, München
First published in England 1978
Fourth impression 1983
Second edition, completely revised, enlarged
and reset, 1984

© THORSONS PUBLISHERS LIMITED 1984

This book is sold subject to the condition that it shall not, by way of trade or otherwise, be lent, re-sold, hired out, or otherwise circulated without the publisher's prior consent in any form, binding, or cover other than that in which it is published and without a similar condition including this condition being imposed on the subsequent purchaser.

British Library Cataloguing in Publication Data

Lutzner, Helmut
  The secrets of successful fasting.—2nd ed.
  Completely rev. enl. & reset
  1. Fasting
  I. Title II. Wie neugeboren durch fasten.
  English
  613.2'5   RM226

ISBN 0-7225-1117-5

Printed in Great Britain by
Richard Clay (The Chaucer Press) Ltd,
Bungay, Suffolk

CONTENTS

	Page
Introduction	7
Chapter	
1. What is Fasting?	9
2. Planning to Fast at Home	18
3. The Right Way to Fast	30
4. Breaking the Fast	53
5. Fasting in a Clinic	62
Index	64

PUBLISHER'S NOTE

This book represents Dr Lützner's successful method of fasting. However, we would draw your attention to Chapter 5 for information on those who should fast only under supervision and those who should avoid fasting altogether.

If you are not in either of these categories and you become concerned, when fasting, about your physical health, we suggest you discuss this with your regular physician or health care practitioner.

INTRODUCTION

This book tells you the truth about fasting: the safest and most effective method of losing weight. To fast is to get rid of poison and waste the natural way, to free yourself from harmful substances that your body may have been harbouring for years. When fasting is combined with a specially-designed programme of exercise and relaxation, it can be one of the most successful ways to health for people with a great variety of illnesses. And think of the other effects of fasting: a clear complexion and healthy hair!

The following pages contain something completely new: the first ever do-it-yourself guide to a week's fasting with day-to-day instructions on how to prepare yourself for the treatment and how to look after yourself during it. Anyone who follows this medically-approved programme can be sure of fasting successfully and without hunger pangs.

CHAPTER ONE
WHAT IS FASTING?

Eating and not eating are like walking and sleeping, tension and relaxation — the poles between which we live our daily lives.

Eating by day and fasting by night belong so naturally to the rhythm of life that we take their existence for granted. But if you happen to eat later than usual in the evening, you may notice the next morning that you are not hungry. This is the body's way of saying that the fasting time is not yet over.

The first meal of the day is not called breakfast for nothing: it is literally the breaking of a night of fasting. If you have not kept your fast the night before, you won't need to break it.

Most people need some twelve to fourteen hours each day to work, play, eat, and interact with others. That leaves ten to twelve hours for the body to recharge its batteries, for wastes to be broken down, and energy to be built up. During the night of fasting the human body looks after itself: it lies still and sleeps. Rest, comfort, and warmth help it to live off its own resources. These are basic requirements for successful fasting, and they will be discussed in detail later in the book.

Fasting and Illness

When ill, a feverish child will refuse food and ask only for refreshing fruit juices. Similarly, a sick dog will crawl into its kennel and eat nothing for days on end. Both know instinctively what is best for them: they fast.

A sick organism needs time to itself to build up its strength. It will get the energy it needs for repair and reconstruction of the damaged parts of its body from its own store of nutrients. Fasting saves the energy demanded daily by the digestive system, which amounts to 30 per cent of the total energy output of the body. This energy goes towards the healing process.

The instinctive fasting that occurs during a fever or other symptoms of illness is really just nature helping itself. It is well known that a high temperature accompanied by natural fasting often wards off lurking disease; together they destroy invading bacteria, control the outbreak or growth of a virus, give increased immunity to the blood and the cells, and step up the elimination of bodily wastes and other poisonous substances.

Fasting and Energy

Despite the popular belief that strength, speed, endurance, and mental concentration all depend on eating enough food, the opposite is true. A German folk expression says, 'A full stomach doesn't like to study'.

What mountaineer would eat before a climb? If he breaks camp at three in the morning he can profit from three, four, or five hours of climbing before breaking his night-time fast. No runner could break a record or ever reach his peak performance if he ate before running.

Thus it should be clear that strength is not derived directly from food as it is eaten but rather from the reserves of foodstuff stored in the body. These reserves first had to undergo the digestive process to be converted into energy. Just ask yourself the following questions: When do I feel particularly energetic? When did I last eat before that time? Did I eat a lot? Little? Practically nothing? Did I take any stimulants, like coffee, black tea, cola, tobacco, alcohol?

A further point to disprove that energy is not obtained *directly* from food: Appetite is absent not only during, but also after, any physical exertion. Thirst demands to be quenched immediately, but hunger asserts itself only much later. People who engage in sports are well aware that accomplishment is connected with not eating and that their energy comes from reserves stored within their own bodies.

During a fast, the transformation of bodily reserves into energy does not sap the body's strength because the body has available to it the energy that would be needed by the digestive system. Thus, maximum energy is available for performance.

It is possible to live for days, even weeks on end, while fasting and still expend awesome amounts of energy. The Swedish doctor, Otto Karl Aly, reports on the marathon hunger march undertaken by twenty of his compatriots who were convinced that the body could not only live off its reserves, but even survive strenuous exercise. The men marched from Göteburg to Stockholm — 300 miles — in ten days, which works out to 30 miles per day, without eating any solid food. They lived entirely on fruit juice and about 3 quarts of water a day. Dr Aly examined them when they reached Stockholm and discovered that, although they had lost eleven to fifteen pounds each, they were in good shape and high spirits and felt not in the least exhausted; on the contrary, their powers of endurance and their strength had increased.

Fasting and Feasting

What would life be like if we couldn't celebrate now and then? Eating is an important part of any celebration. The trouble is that often we don't eat just to satisfy our hunger and our bodily needs: we gorge ourselves. Eating becomes pure luxury. The needs we are satisfying are purely social and sensual — the pleasure of the company of others, the enjoyment of new tastes. It is a game played with knife, fork, and glass.

Whatever the next day brings, whether it's a hangover, a queasy stomach or just a loss of appetite, this is the ideal time to begin a fast, to let the body get back to normal. Why do we never listen to what our bodies tell us? The most natural thing to do after over-eating and drinking is to stop eating altogether until you get hungry again, which might be anything from a few hours to a day or more.

Alternative Energy Programmes

The body has two energy programmes. One is based on the intake of food, the other on the body's reserves:

1. *Energy from Food*
   Food ⟶ Digestion ⟶ Conversion of foodstuffs into energy ⟶ Excretion
   Result: strength and warmth
2. *Energy from the Body's Reserves*
   Stores of fat and protein ⟶ Inner digestion ⟶ Conversion into energy ⟶ Excretion
   Result: strength and warmth

The body's switch-over from producing energy from food to producing energy from its own reserves and vice versa is completely automatic. Psychologically, the switch-over from the fasting programme is facilitated by the knowledge that there is a built-in ability for the body to provide energy during a fast, that fasting is not dangerous, and that the decision to fast has been entirely voluntary.

The person fasting for the first time will be suprised to discover that he is not hungry and that he feels well and energetic. The experience gives him confidence that his body knows what it is doing. The discovery that life without food is possible gives the faster that inner assurance that is always admired by those who have never tried fasting themselves.

Defeating Hunger

Hunger is the body's way of saying that it is producing saliva and digestive juices and is ready to take in food. If the energy supply is not revitalized by food, the hunger signal will grow stronger, eventually reaching that unpleasant pitch where we refer to ourselves as 'starving', and we suffer from gnawing pains in the stomach that we just cannot ignore. In this state the circulation may react and cause dizziness, nausea, and weakness, sometimes even sweating and trembling. A glass of fruit juice can take the edge off this sort of acute hunger for a short while, but the only way to satisfy it for longer is to eat.

It is worth noting here that hunger is not always a craving for food; it can be the expression of a craving for love or for comfort, of a desire for recognition from others, or for self-assertion. Countless people are overweight or unbalanced metabolically because they make subconscious efforts to satisfy themselves psychologically by eating, drinking, or smoking.

It is easier to understand why the faster does not get hungry when you realize that his metabolism has switched over on to the second energy programme. He is not hungry because he is being satisfied by his inner energy source. As long as his body has reserves of strength he will be able to fast. The internal organs of a healthy person function as safely and naturally as they would do normally.

Learning to Fast

Everybody has a capacity to switch his metabolism over on to the second energy programme. It is a fresh experience that everyone can learn to practise. It is, of course, much easier for the body that is used to fasting to switch over to the second programme in the absence of food than it is for the body that has never fasted. Skipping a meal is no longer a problem if you are used to fasting. It is even possible to assume a position halfway between the two programmes — to live on a reduced diet and to derive energy partly from food and partly from the body's reserves — without experiencing hunger. This is what happens when food intake is gradually built up after a short fast. A good rule to remember is: fasting is not starving. If you feel you are 'starving' you are not fasting.

By now it should be clear that fasting is a natural process. It is strange that so few people seem to realize this and that the suggestion that it is possible to live without food — and live actively — is absolutely incomprehensible to them. They are afraid of doing without, of getting ill, even dying. This is the sort of prejudice that is very deep-rooted and hard to eradicate. But you need only to look around you, at nature, to learn the truth.

Fasting in the Animal World

Many animals in their natural state fast for weeks or even months as a normal part of their yearly routine. This is nature's way of helping them to survive the season when their food supply ceases to exist. Highland animals like the ibex, chamois, deer, and marmot fatten themselves in autumn so that they will have a good store of food for the winter. But while the marmot is in hibernation, thus needing very little energy to survive, ibex, chamois, and deer continue to battle against snow and bitter cold. The fact that their mating season, with its fierce fights between males, occurs during this period of fasting, should be enough to convince even the sceptic that fasting in no way diminishes potency; in this case it would seem to increase it.

Something similar can be observed in the life of the fish. During the whole of its long, strenuous journey up-river and the subsequent spawning season, the salmon eats nothing. It is also known that wolves can go long stretches and cover long distances without food. Migratory birds eat more than they need during the second half of the summer, thereby doubling their normal weight. With the extra fuel, they are able to fly up to 3,000 miles. After this feat, their weight returns to normal. Almost all animals of prey eat whenever they make a kill and live in the absence of food on the nutrients stored within their bodies.

The Roots of Human Fasting

Like animals, humans are born with the ability to live on foodstuffs stored in the body, an ability which is biologically necessary for survival. Whole races would have died out without it.

It is possible to survive long after all sources of food have dried up, even after the body's reserves have been broken down. It takes a very long time for a human being to die of starvation. Fasting is a natural course of events for man — one which he can take for granted and at the same time use to his advantage.

Primitive tribes in Australia and Africa live today as they have for thousands of years in their barren surroundings, times of plenty alternating with times of famine.

The story of the ancient Hunza tribe is a good illustration of the fact that fasting gives more energy than just that needed to survive. The tribe lives in a high valley in the Central Himalayas. Only a couple of hundred years ago it was completely isolated from the outside world, almost hermetically sealed off. Dr Ralph Bircher writes in his book, *The Hunzas,* of the astonishing fact that the valley slopes could not produce enough food to feed the people the whole year round. Until May, when the grain was ripe, the whole tribe would fast for up to two months. The Hunzas remained happy and contented and able to do the work required of them at that particular season of the year: they cultivated the fields and repaired their irrigation systems. They had no doctor and they needed no police force. Their lives were played out to completely natural laws.

Now the valley has been made accessible. The men of the Hunza tribe serve as soldiers in India, or have other jobs outside their settlement. Staple foods that can be stored easily, like sugar, flour, and preserves are imported; the tribe need no longer 'starve'. But now the Hunzas are victims of typical diseases of civilization: tooth decay, appendicitis, gall stones, overweight, colds and diabetes, to name but a few. Not only do they need a doctor, they need police as well. The health of their bodies and minds and their natural behaviour have been destroyed.

The example of the Hunzas can perhaps help to clarify the reasons behind religious fasting. Man thanks his god for the fact that he can survive and be happy. Fasting can be the way to inner peace, finding your own direction in life and your individuality. The great leaders of the world — Moses, Christ, Buddha, and Mohammed — probably found the key to existence during periods of fasting.

Who today, surrounded by plenty, can understand the deeper meaning of fasting in solitude, of the voluntary renunciation of our daily bread?

If someone were to prevent you from eating, against your own will, you would feel hungry and would rebel. Even the Church has been divided during its fasts. Whenever religious fasts have been decreed, people have gone against them, either privately or publicly. Some of the more recent objections have been on the grounds of health. Only the bare bones are left of these religious occasions. All the spirit has gone.

We should make it one of our most important aims to discover the real value of fasting for ourselves. Nothing can be of greater help to a person than to discover something for himself, and fasting is an experience that is intensely personal; it can be done only on your own. Remember that fasting is not starvation; it has nothing to do with deprivation; it does not mean eating less or just going, say, without meat on Friday. Fasting is not fanaticism, and it is not necessarily tied to religious practices. Fasting is a natural part of human life; it is living off nutrients stored in the body. Fasting means that the body has the strength to look after itself from its own resources.

The prerequisites of fasting are: a mind open to trying new things, the readiness to try fasting, and the determination to stick to it.

The Four Basic Rules of Fasting

1. *Eat nothing:* for one, two, or more weeks. You can drink tea, vegetable broth, fruit or vegetable juices, and as much water as it takes to quench your thirst.
2. *Give up everything not necessary for life:* that is, everything that has become a habit to you that might harm the body during the fasting period: every form of nicotine and alcohol; sweeteners of all kinds; coffee; and drugs, as far as you can, especially diuretics, diet pills, and laxatives.
3. *Get rid of everyday concerns:* free yourself from professional and family ties. Put aside your telephone and date book. Don't read magazines, listen to the radio, or watch television. Instead of relying on stimuli from the outside, try living with yourself; instead of relying upon other people and outside circumstances to give you your direction in life, let yourself be directed from within.
4. *Behave naturally:* do whatever does your body good. If your body asks you to do something, do it. If you are exhausted, then sleep yourself out. If you like physical activity, engage in any sport you like — hiking, swimming, whatever you enjoy. Do the things that please you — reading, dancing, listening to music, pursuing your hobby.

Different Kinds of Fasting
Four kinds of fasting are:
1. *Water fasting:* pure spring or mineral water — as much and as often as wanted.

This zero-calorie diet is usually carried out in a hospital where vitamins and mineral tablets are usually given.

2. *Tea fasting:* assorted herbal teas taken three times a day — without honey.

A tea fast also is without calories but has the advantage of allowing warm drinks.

3. *Broth-porridge fasting:* this kind of fast is particularly indicated for people with sensitive stomachs or intestines and will be discussed later (p. 27).

4. *Tea-broth-juice fasting:* herb teas, hot vegetable broths, and fruit and vegetable juices.

This combination fast has been used for decades by tens of thousands of patients with proven outstanding success at the famous Buchinger fasting "clinic" in Southern Germany. I recommend it as the most appropriate for an independent fast.

How to Get Around to an Independent Fast
Take every opportunity you can in your daily life to put yourself on the road to fasting.

Never force yourself to eat when you don't really feel hungry. For example, many people don't feel hungry in the morning. If that is so in your case, just don't eat until lunch; that would be a 'morning fast'.

Fast whenever you have over-eaten, after big holiday feasts, when your stomach is upset or you have diarrhoea. Continue the fast until the natural feeling of hunger comes back.

Fast whenever you have a fever, influenza, tonsilitis, or bronchitis. Plan to work a short fast — 5 days — into your next vacation or easy work week.

What You Can Achieve Through Fasting
Weight Loss: fasting is the quickest, most painless, and least dangerous way of losing those extra pounds.

Internal Cleansing: fasting relieves the body of excess and toxic matter.

Purification: fasting is one of the few successful natural purifiers in a polluted world. It can help in overcoming drug addiction and dependence on alcohol and cigarettes.

Clear Skin: fasting is a beauty treatment from within.

Rejuvenation: fasting helps to keep you young and to give you physical and psychological energy. During the years of 'the change,' for men and women it can help to prevent loss of sexual energy.

Prevention: fasting is a powerful preventive force against disease.

Cure: fasting is the most effective and least dangerous cure for anyone with any form of digestive complaint. A long fast has long been known as the 'royal road to healing' for many illnesses, both chronic and acute.

Please don't confuse a healing fast with the week's fast described in this book! A healing fast will be discussed briefly in the last chapter. A week of fasting was chosen as the shortest time in which it would be possible to learn something about fasting and to get some idea of the results you could get from a real healing fast (two to four weeks). It is best to start with small steps.

To take the plunge and embark on your first fast you need no more than curiosity and the courage to try out a new experience.

CHAPTER TWO
PLANNING TO FAST AT HOME

Fasting is not harmful in any way, if you are reasonably fit and active and have the self-control to stick to your intentions. (Old people and young people over the age of fourteen as well as the handicapped can all fast safely at home, as long as their bodies function normally.) It is also safe for healthy, pregnant women to fast — but for no longer than a week.

When Is It Best Not to Fast at Home?
If, even after reading this book, you still have your doubts about fasting.

If you are suffering from severe depression.

If you are still in a state of physical weakness after an operation.

If you are under stress, exhausted, or suffering from nervous tension. Wait until you feel better before you begin fasting.

If you are dependent on a programme of prescribed drugs which must be strictly followed.

If you are in poor health, suffering from a chronic illness or from high or low blood-pressure. Consult a doctor before beginning to fast at home.

What Is the Best Way to Fast?
The easiest way is to fast in a group of like-minded people. Fasting can be an exhilarating experience if it is undertaken with a group of friends. However, each member of the group should have a private place to which he can withdraw to be alone, meeting with the others regularly to discuss progress and enjoy some form of group activity.

A group of people fasting will find that they can share a great diversity of experiences and draw closer to one another, certainly give one another confidence and help. Before the week of fasting begins, you may feel like consulting a doctor experienced in this area who would be willing to monitor the group throughout the fast.

If you prefer to fast alone with your partner, you will experience the same advantages as you would with a group, only on a smaller scale. Living through a fast together, you will learn to stand outside yourselves and look at each other with different eyes. The help and encouragement you give each other is bound to deepen your relationship. Here again, it is important that both partners be alone and undisturbed when they wish.

Fasting alone is more difficult. Solitary fasting demands great discipline and self control on the part of the individual, who must be capable of renunciation and self-contentment at the same time. If you manage to fast alone successfully for a week, you can be proud of yourself.

What Is the Best Place to Fast?
Anywhere, familiar to you, where you would be comfortable and warm and feel at home, would be suitable. It could be in your own home, the home of friends, a holiday home, a mountain chalet, aboard a sailing boat, or in a tent in your back yard.

You can fast anywhere you enjoy being — where you can play your favourite sport or just laze around, if that is what suits you best. In other words, it is up to you.

It is important to choose a place where you will have peace and quiet and time to be on your own. You want to be free of pressure, free of deadlines. If you are fasting, you will often just want to withdraw into your own shell.

Fasting at Home
If you choose to fast at home, you must take into account the fact that this is the place where your eating and drinking habits are at their strongest. You will be reminded of them by the people and things around you. There are a thousand invisible threads which join you to your everyday life, and these will tug at you every time you pass through the kitchen, see the refrigerator, the dining table, the liquor cabinet. And the worst thing about fasting at home, the one disadvantage you should be prepared to handle is the ready advice of friends and neighbours who drop in and say, 'Oh, I wouldn't do that, I read in the paper recently...' or, 'Go on, I'm sure one wouldn't hurt you! You'll starve yourself to death if you continue like that!'

It is far less disturbing for the faster to be in a house where food is being cooked as usual and children are coming home hungry from school than it is to contend with well-meaning advice and offers of help from those who just don't understand.

So, in general, home is not always the best place to fast, but it is up to you to choose the place where you feel most comfortable and at ease, and if this place is your home, then you should fast there. If that is how you feel, then your fast will be a successful one.

When Is the Best Time to Fast?
Decide well in advance when you are going to fast. Ideally it should coincide with a week away from work. Failing this, try to arrange it so that your professional life is not too demanding that week and that you will be able to put off all social commitments.

Fasting on Vacation
Fasting and freedom seem to go together naturally. In fact, freedom from everyday pressures and duties, from bustle and noise, is essential for a successful fast.

Why not have a fasting holiday! Experienced fasters know that this is the best time to fast — the time when the nervous system switches off and retires from the rat race. Such freedom from nervous preoccupation is the best guarantee of success.

Workday Fasting
It is quite possible to fast in the normal course of everyday life; many people do so successfully. But if you are too fast and carry on working at the same time you will need more discipline and self-assurance. Anyone who has fasted before, however briefly, will know his own capabilities.

As a doctor experienced in fasting, I feel I ought to warn the first-time faster not to mix fasting with his everyday life because he will be making it much harder for himself. Apart from the countless temptations he will be exposed to all the time and the doubts of his colleagues who will try to shake his confidence, there are other things he needs to be careful about: the rhythm of life during fasting is slowed down; everything you do will take longer; the circulation is not as stable as usual, admittedly, only for a few hours each day, but who can guarantee that no extra demands will be made on you during that time?

The faster is, alas, usually more sensitive and vulnerable to comment and abuse by others. Lastly, if you drive a car you should take into account that your reactions will not be as quick as usual, nor your concentration as great.

On no account should you fast while you are working if you have a career that makes heavy demands on you, if your work involves responsibility for others, or if you are involved with machinery that could harm you or others.

Special Rules for Workday Fasting
Allow more time that you usually do for getting washed and dressed in the morning and for your morning exercises. This might mean getting up earlier! Allow more time for your trip to work. Don't hurry — and do leave your car at home. Go by bus or train and get out before your normal stop so you can walk the rest of the way. Walk up the stairs instead of taking the elevator. Movement and fresh air are all important. Use the lunch break for a walk in the park or a snooze in your chair or for stretching out on the floor.

Be aware of the different smell of your breath and your body. Rinse out your mouth regularly with fresh water or a mouth wash and give up sugar in drinks. On your days off you can join in with other people and do everything they do, but make sure that you go to bed early and that you are not burdened with visitors and invitations. Get together regularly with other fasters and keep in contact with them whenever possible.

Who Can Advise You While You Fast
If you are afraid that you are not quite fit, then have a word with your doctor beforehand. During the fast you will find that any doctor who has experience in this area will be only too glad to help.

Anyone who has ever fasted before will be able to give you help and support of a non-medical kind. It is all a question of mutual trust. The most important thing is that you always try to share your experiences ; it is always reassuring to have someone to turn to who has gone through what you are going through and can be of assistance if necessary.

Getting Ready For Fasting
Shopping
What you will need for the first six days:
3 pounds (1.3 kg) fruit for a fruit day *or*
3 pounds raw vegetables for a raw vegetable day *or*
6 oz/170g (⅔ cupful) brown rice for a rice day
½ lb/225 g (1 cupful) crushed flaxseed

5-10 bottles of non-sparkling mineral water, spring water or other pure water

15 tea bags of assorted herb teas. Mild black tea or ginseng tea if you have a tendency to low blood-pressure

2 × ½ pints/285ml (1 ⅓ cupsful) of your favourite fruit juice or assorted fruit juices

2 × ½ pints/285ml (1 ⅓ cupsful) of your favourite vegetable juice or assorted vegetable juices

3 tablespoonsful Glauber salts, (sodium sulphate) from your pharmacist

4 tablespoonsful Epsom salts, (magnesium sulphate) if you don't want to take enemas.

(Leave the shopping for your gradual build-up towards normal eating until the last day of your fast. Then you will find it pleasant to shop and to look forward to eating again.)

Start With a Clean Slate

Clear up all chores and duties still outstanding. Eat as you would normally. Do not attempt to fatten yourself up. There is no need.

Give away all your perishable food, put the rest under lock and key, and give the key to a friend or neighbour.

What to Have at Hand

Warmer clothing than normal for the time of year.
Enough underwear for more frequent changes than normal.
Sports equipment.
Enema kit.
Skin oil.
Dry skin brush.

The Day Before

1. *Basic rule: Eat little!*

Include in your diet for this day plenty of raw fruits or vegetables. It is a good idea to take a tablespoonful of crushed flaxseed mixed with yogurt or apple sauce, three times during the day. This will bind together the poisons and waste in the intestines. Here are three sample menus for the day before that are especially good if you are overweight (you can use them now and also later whenever you want to lose two to three pounds quickly).

Fruit Day:
3 pounds (1.3kg) fruit during the day, divided into three meals. Don't forget to chew well!

Salad Day:
In the morning fruit, fruit salad or granola. At midday and in the evening, a vegetable plate — any leafy greens and/or grated vegetables, but not with mayonnaise. Use a dressing of oil, lemon juice, and herbs.

Rice day:
Three meals, each consisting of 4 tablespoonful rice (preferably brown), boiled in water without salt. Eat it in the morning and in the evening with a stewed apple or apple sauce and at midday with two stewed tomatoes seasoned with herbs.

2. *No cigarettes, alcohol, coffee, sweets.* Don't panic — it will only be for a week.

3. *Prepare yourself psychologically.* Read any available book on fasting. If possible talk to people who have had personal experience with fasting.

4. *Start your fasting diary* (p. 40). The physical changeover from eating to fasting has already begun. It can help, at this point, to give yourself some reinforcing thoughts:

I have made up my mind to fast, and I know I can do it.
I have left all my daily concerns behind me.
Finally I have time for myself.
I have everything I need: a few liquid foods, water, and a good internal supply of nourishment.
I am anxious to see the result of this experience but I have no qualms. I shall be following nature's way, and that cannot be bad.

PLAN FOR THE FASTING WEEK

Day of Preparation	Shopping for the fast Settling outstanding business	Letting go of everyday concerns
The Day Before Morning	Fruit and nuts or granola	Wind down and get some rest
Midday	Raw vegetable salad, potatoes and other vegetables, cottage cheese dessert	
Afternoon	One apple	
Evening	Fruit or fruit salad, yogurt, one crispbread	Read your book on fasting

First Day of Fasting Morning	Thorough elimination with Glauber salt or enema	Stay at home
Midday	Vegetable broth or vegetable cocktail	Take a nap while keeping warm
Afternoon	Herb tea (with a teaspoonful of honey)	
Evening	Fruit or vegetable juice or vegetable broth	
Second Day of Fasting Morning	Herb tea (with a teaspoonful of honey)	Keep active
Midday	Potato broth	Take a nap, while keeping warm
Afternoon	Herb tea (with a teaspoonful of honey)	
Evening	Fruit or vegetable juice or vegetable broth	Make a warm compress for the abdomen
Third Day of Fasting Morning	Herb tea (with a teaspoonful of honey)	Get plenty of exercise. Take an enema or Epsom salts.
Midday	Carrot broth	Take a nap while keeping warm
Afternoon	Herb tea (with a teaspoonful of honey)	
Evening	Fruit or vegetable juice or vegetable broth	Read your book on fasting
Fourth Day of Fasting Morning	Herb tea (with a teaspoonful of honey)	Get exercise
Midday	Vegetable broth or vegetable cocktail	Take a nap while keeping warm
Afternoon	Herb tea (with a teaspoonful of honey)	
Evening	Fruit or vegetable juice or vegetable broth	

Fifth Day of Fasting		
Morning	Herb tea (with a teaspoonful of honey)	Shop for the return to eating
Midday	Celery broth	Take an enema or Epsom salts. Take a nap while keeping warm
Afternoon	Herb tea (with a teaspoonful of honey)	Read rules about beginning to eat
Evening	Fruit or vegetable juice or vegetable broth	
First Day of Eating		
Morning	Morning tea, if desired, one apple or apple sauce	Take your time, eat slowly, and enjoy!
Midday	Potato soup	Take a nap while keeping warm
Afternoon	One apple or apple sauce	
Evening	Vegetable soup, yogurt, crispbread	Put dried fruit in water to soak
Second Day of Eating		
Morning	Soaked prunes, figs, bread, butter	Continue to eat slowly
Midday	Raw vegetable salad, baked potatoes, vegetables, cottage cheese	Take a nap while keeping warm
Afternoon	Apple, hazelnuts	
Evening	Tomatoes, wholewheat bread, butter, cream cheese, crispbread	Take an enema or Epsom salts

The First Day of Fasting

It is most advisable to start your fast with empty bowels. If you have regular bowel movements, this should be no problem at all; it will happen in the natural course of events, and you will need no laxatives. However, as statistics show, only about 30 per cent of the population has completely regular bowel movements; the remaining 70 per cent all suffer from some difficulty or other. It is a good idea to hurry the process along by drinking a glass of buttermilk first thing in the morning.

It is recommended also that the following laxative be taken: dissolve 3 tablespoonsful of Glauber salt in 3 cupsful of warm water. Mix 2 tablespoonsful in 2 cupsful for small people. Drink this within 15 minutes. You can disguise the taste if you like by following it up quickly with fruit juice or syrup.

After you have drunk this, the bowel will take from one to three hours to empty itself, probably in a number of diarrhoea-like movements. If you are very constipated, this could take until the afternoon, so you will obviously want to stay close to a toilet.

If you anticipate any disorders of the stomach or if you are very slender, it is best to avoid Glauber salt. Instead, give yourself an enema (you'll learn how on p. 31). It is an equally good way to begin your fast.

Important: If you should get stomach cramps, lie down in bed with a hot water bottle. Make sure that your feet are warm — put a second hot water bottle on them if they are not. Should you get very thirsty, drink peppermint tea or water.

Women who take an oral contraceptive in the morning should not take it until at least three hours after taking the laxative, lest it be eliminated with the emptying of the bowels. An enema should not necessitate any change.

The fast begins when the intestines are empty. The body has switched over from eating to fasting and begins to live on its inner reserves. You are no longer hungry. You are living on your own.

It is best to spend the day at home, or in your chosen fasting resort. If you feel like lying down, do so; otherwise, just relax, read, go for a short walk, but do nothing strenuous. Avoid hot baths and saunas.

Menu for all Fasting Days

Morning: 1 or 2 cupsful of herb tea or mild black tea or ginseng tea; with 1 teaspoonful of honey and/or lemon if desired.
Between times: Plenty of pure spring or mineral water, occasionally with a squeeze of lemon.
Noon: 1 cupful freshly-made vegetable broth (see recipes p. 27) or 1 cupful fresh vegetable juice or 1 cupful bottled vegetable juice diluted with pure water. These may be taken hot or cold.
Afternoon: 1 or 2 cupsful of herb tea or mild black tea (not after 4 o'clock) with a teaspoonful of honey and/or lemon.

Evening: 1 cupful hot vegetable broth, as at noon, or fruit or vegetable juice, hot or cold, diluted with pure water.

BROTH RECIPES
(For 4 people)

POTATO BROTH
2 cupsful water
2 potatoes, unpeeled
2 carrots
1 leek stalk
Small bunch parsley
1 celery stalk
1 teaspoonful caraway seeds
1 teaspoonful marjoram

Wash, dice, and simmer all the ingredients 10 to 20 minutes. Put through sieve. Add sea salt, oat flakes, grated nutmeg, dill, or basil. The herbs are important to make the broth tasty.

CARROT BROTH
2 cupsful water
2 large carrots, unpeeled
1 leek stalk
Small bunch parsley
1 celery stalk

Prepare as above.

CELERY BROTH
2 cupsful water
2 large celery stalks
1 leek and 1 carrot

Prepare as above.

TOMATO BROTH
2 cupsful water
3 tomatoes
1 clove garlic
1 leek, 1 celery stalk, 1 carrot
Oregano or marjoram, to taste

Prepare as above, but simmer only for 5 to 10 minutes. Add tomato paste to taste.

RECIPES
(For 1 person)

OAT PORRIDGE
Cook 3 tablespoonsful oat flakes cooked in 2 cupsful of water. Strain, pour into thermos bottle, and drink slowly chewing each mouthful before swallowing.

RICE PORRIDGE
Cook 2 tablespoonsful rice in 2 cupsful of water. Proceed as above.

FLAXSEED PORRIDGE
Cook 2-3 tablespoonsful flaxseed in 2 cupsful water in a deep pot. After five minutes of cooking, let the pot stand undisturbed for a few minutes until the porridge can be easily seperated from the foam. Strain off the foam. Use only half the porridge.

Oat, rice, or flaxseed porridge can be enriched with yeast extracts, honey, or vegetable and fruit juices to taste.

All fasting drinks should be drunk one mouthful at a time, 'chewing' each mouthful. Warm it or cool it in the mouth before swallowing. Enjoy! Drink slowly!.

These drinks provide vitamins, minerals, alkaline substances, and easily-utilized carbohydrates, which counteract the overacidity of the stomach during a fast.

Drink as much water as you like throughout the fast. Indeed, drink more rather than less than you need to quench your thirst. Water plays an important part in "washing out" the toxins from the system.

If you don't like or don't tolerate concentrated fruit or vegetable juices, dilute them with water or stir in one teaspoonful of flaxseed; the fine mucilagenous flaxseed binds the fruit and vegetable acids.

People with sensitive stomachs fast best with oat, rice or flaxseed porridge. (Recipes above.) In case of stomach problems it helps to take a swallow of diluted porridge also at night or in the morning. (It would be good to keep some on hand and warm in a thermos bottle.)

The Second Day of Fasting
On the second day, your body will still be getting used to not receiving food, and you might still feel a few hunger pangs. Half a glass of water will still them. On no account should you take

drugs or slimming pills to drive away your appetite. During this time the blood-pressure will be falling and you may be feeling a little nauseous or dizzy, but this is harmless and will pass quite quickly, especially if you take a walk in the fresh air or splash your face with cold water — both help quickly. If necessary lie down briefly.

Many fasters are overcome at this time by a sort of spiritual hangover. They are filled with doubts and start wondering whether they have taken on too much. The remedy is to do something to cheer yourself up, anything that you normally find enlivening in times of depression. Do not force yourself into anything, but, on the other hand, don't let yourself get bogged down with worries and fears.

Take great care on this second fast day to keep well away from temptation: give food stores, restaurants, and generous friends a wide berth.

Most fasters will find by the end of the second day that they have become used to the idea of not eating, but some are still struggling into their third day. It is always possible that you will experience a sudden hunger pang or a longing for a little something, but you must be firm with yourself and resist. Drink as much water as you like.

If you really have to contend with unbearable hunger pangs, then get rid of them once and for all with a tablespoonful of Glauber salt or Epsom salt dissolved in a large glass of warm water, or drink a few sips of buttermilk. An enema can be helpful here, too.

The Third, Fourth and Fifth Days of Fasting

On the third, fourth and fifth fast days you will be more stable, confident, and assured. You will have realized how well the body can look after itself and how naturally it has made the change from eating to fasting. By this stage you will be able to do everything that you can normally do.

However, there are many points on which you will need a little more guidance, and below you will find a list of helpful tips. It is the normal everyday things that will change when you fast; things like getting up, going to the toilet, rest, exercise, warmth, and sleep: they all undergo a change which you will need help to deal with.

CHAPTER THREE
THE RIGHT WAY TO FAST

Although the faster's circulation is functioning properly, it is not functioning as quickly as usual. If you spring energetically out of bed in the morning you could find yourself lying down again pretty quickly feeling sick and dizzy with everything turning black before your eyes. You will have to learn to do it differently: while you are still in bed, stretch your legs and arms and arch your back like a cat. Next, swing yourself slowly into a sitting position on the edge of the bed; then stand up slowly. Splash your face with cold water.

If you want to be a little more adventurous, here are three suggestions: wash your whole body from head to foot in cold water and then quickly get back into bed again without drying yourself. Or, take a quick, cold shower, then go back to bed. Or, after a warm shower, let cold water run over your arms and legs, starting from your toes to your knees and from your fingertips to your elbows. Or, if it is cold, take a brisk run outside, then slip back into bed and enjoy the warmth creeping back over you.

Do not take strenuous exercise; do just enough to wake up tired limbs, stretch the muscles, straighten a stiff back, and get the circulation going. You might enjoy doing it all to music. In short, it should be relaxed, playful, like a game. Take an air bath: stand naked at an open window and with a bath brush or towel give your body a good rub down all over, starting with the tips of your fingers and toes. Do this until you feel warm, about 10 to 15 minutes.

After you have taken a bath, rub your body with herbal oil.

Getting Rid of Bodily Waste
All the ducts of the body will be open during fasting and will purge themselves of the metabolic waste that has been collecting there for years. The cleansing of the body is by no means over with the emptying of the bowels on the first day. Food is brought into the intestines and waste expelled from them. During the fast the intestines are performing only half their normal function:

expelling waste. To do this successfully during a fast requires an enema every second day.

How to Give Yourself an Enema

Take the enema bag (basically it is a syringe with a squeezy rubber sack at the end) and fill it with water. Squeeze it out in the toilet or washbasin until all the air bubbles have been expelled from the tube. Put a peg in the tube or, if there is one, turn the screw to stop the water flowing out. Rub a little vaseline round the end of the tube. Now hang the bag from a hook on the wall or the door handle or window catch, squat down on the floor with your knees and elbows on the ground and insert the end of the tube into the anus. Allow the water to flow freely into the rectum as you kneel on the floor. Relax and breathe naturally. In two to five minutes you will feel an urgent need to use the toilet, where all the water inside you will flush out the residue from the intestines in a couple of sharp bursts.

Admittedly, giving yourself an enema may not be very pleasant, but it is the least harmful and most effective way of emptying the bowel, and the faster will feel a great relief and release from hunger pangs after using it. It is also a good way to treat a host of other pains during fasting — headaches, for example.

If you don't want to use an enema, you can drink 2 teaspoonsful of Epsom salt dissolved in a glass (1 cupful) of warm water first thing in the morning. A small glass (½ cupful) of sauerkraut juice or buttermilk in the morning can also help, but it is up to the individual to find out what suits him best, always bearing in mind that commercially sold laxatives can be harmful to you while fasting.

Excretion does not stop with fasting; faeces will be passed even after 20 days without food.

The Urine

If your urine becomes very dark in colour and has a strong odour, it is advisable to drink more water than you need merely to quench your thirst. Water is the ideal cleanser for the kidneys and the urinary tracts. Sometimes you will pass a lot of water and sometimes only a little. Never resort to diuretics, as these can only destroy the delicate balance created by your own body and will do infinitely more harm than good.

The Skin

During a fast the skin will give off more odours than usual, which will give you some idea of the impurities that are secreted with sweat and end up in the laundry basket each week. For this reason it will be necessary to change your underwear frequently. Make sure that the fabric is soft and absorbent. It should not be synthetic.

Frequent washing, showering, or bathing obviously are indispensible to the faster. Always be sure to wash before a sauna or a swim. You may find that your skin is getting drier; this can be corrected by rubbing in a herbal oil (from your pharmacy or health food store) after each wash.

While you are fasting you should never use make-up, face cream, or powder, as these clog up the pores and make it difficult for the skin to breathe or get rid of impurities. If you must use a deodorant, use it sparingly to safeguard against skin irritations.

Do look forward to the smooth, clear skin you will have when the fast is over!

The Lungs

The air that you breathe out is full of gaseous metabolic waste, which is all right as long as you are outside in the fresh air. However, if you are indoors remember to air the room thoroughly each hour by throwing open the windows for a good five minutes. At night you should turn off the heating and sleep with the window open.

The Mucous Membranes

The mucous membranes in the nose and throat usually clean themselves. The fresh morning air stimulates spitting, nose-blowing, throat-clearing. A few splashes of cold water on the face can produce the same effect.

During the fast there will be more phlegm than usual, but, if not aggravated, any irritation caused by smoking stands a good chance of disappearing by the end of the week. Therefore, it is essential that you stick to your intention of giving up cigarettes while you fast. Chewing gum or peppermint tablets can help overcome that 'empty mouth' feeling.

The Vagina

The vagina cleans itself just as do the nose and throat. So during the fasting period there may be more vaginal discharge than usual.

The Mouth
Your tongue will turn a yellowish grey, or even brown or black, depending on the type of waste your body is getting rid of. Teeth and gums will smell and taste less pleasant than usual. Use your toothbrush on your tongue as well as your teeth and gums, and rinse out your mouth with water whenever you feel like it, or suck on a lemon. The glands in your mouth are also involved in expelling waste, but if the smell becomes too unpleasant you should consult your pharmacist, who will recommend a suitable mouthwash.

Spiritual Waste
You will find that you are getting rid of spiritual as well as bodily waste. There is nothing to worry about if you start to have violent dreams about war, sex, bloodshed and perversion. Neither should you be bothered by unnatural thoughts or feelings of aggression or desperation. The important thing is to be able to talk about what is troubling you. If you have no one in whom you can confide, you should write down your impressions and read them over to yourself when the mood has passed. Whatever you do about it, you will have to come to terms with this spiritual residue, and once you have done so it will be as great a relief as getting rid of your body's impurities.

How Much Can the Faster Take On?
The amount of energy you have while fasting does not depend so much on the fast itself as on how much energy you have normally. You have a ready supply of energy within you which will enable you to do as much as you usually do. An elderly person will probably prefer to make walking his exercise. A normal adult who is not trained in sports will find that he has enough energy to work in the garden, provided that he takes it slowly and rhythmically.

There are, however, a few small differences which it is as well to be aware of. Anything that requires a combination of strength and speed, like running up the stairs, football, skiing, etc., will be found more of a strain than usual. It is better to choose an activity that requires endurance rather than sudden effort. Swimming, walking, slow hill-climbing, cycling, rowing, and callisthenics are all suitable sports.

Whatever activity you choose, it is important that you exercise daily to your full capacity. If you want to set yourself a keep-fit course with the object of increasing your physical ability, there is absolutely no reason why you should not do it during your fast, providing that: you have a regular daily practice session; you are exercising all your muscles; you exercise to your maximum capacity at least twice a day; you take things gradually; you alternate smoothly between activity and relaxation.

If you train in this way, you will strengthen your muscles and lose weight at the same time. Although this may seem paradoxical, it is not: The muscles get bigger with use, while the fat is broken down to power them with energy. If you lie in bed while you fast you will feel as bad as you would if you remained totally inactive while eating. You would lose strength and suppleness, just as if you were confined to a hospital bed. It is true that lazy and inactive people lose just as much weight as energetic ones, but their muscles necessarily suffer as well as their fat — both are broken down together — and then they wonder why they feel weak and drained when they come off the fast!

The examples set by two fasters are worth recording here. A 49-year-old Swiss 10,000-metre runner trained every day during his fast. On the 49th day he ran the best time he had ever run.

A sports-playing 40-year old fasted for 21 days and lost 24 pounds. Each day he did exercises, played tennis, swam and walked for hours. After the fast he was in the best of health. A year later he fasted for the same amount of time, but this time his leg was in a plaster cast due to an accident and he had to remain inactive, apart from some simple exercises in his room. After the 21 days had passed he had again lost 24 pounds, but this time he was weak and out of condition, and when his cast was taken off he had to learn to walk again. It took him six weeks to get back into top form.

Of course, when you fast you can be as mentally active as ever, and it is an ideal opportunity to take up some artistic or creative work, which will often turn out surprisingly well. An Austrian philosopher admitted to me that he wrote his best pieces while fasting. Several painters have told me that fasting gave them a depth of perception in tone and colour they had never experienced before.

While you are fasting you can treat yourself to a massage, bathe in sea and sun, and even take a sauna, provided your circulation is giving you no problems and you allow yourself only two temperature changes in ten minutes. On leaving the sauna, promptly splash cold water on your face with both hands!

Resting Three Times a Day
The quicker you allow your body to find a natural rhythm between tension and relaxation, movement and rest, the better you will feel both physically and mentally.

After every form of physical activity, whether it be a bath, a sauna, a massage, or anything else, you should take a rest. This doesn't mean sit down with a book. Close your eyes, let out a deep breath and relax. Give your metabolism time to do its work. It is constantly breaking down, transforming, building up the body cells; to do this it needs complete relaxation. If you are able to rest only once during the day, make it at midday. Lie flat on your back with a partly-full hot water bottle or with a warm compression on your stomach with a steaming towel. The idea of this is to aid the liver in its important work of detoxication. Merely lying down will increase the flow of blood through the liver by 40 per cent; applying heat will help even more. It does not matter where you lie down, in bed, on the couch, on a soft carpet, or on the grass. The important thing is that you lie flat, that you relax, and that you keep warm.

A Word About Relaxation
Once you have learned to let go and relax, everything will be so much easier for you. Fasting makes the body naturally inclined to rest, and this is when yoga, breath control, or any other physical discipline that teaches you to relax and concentrate on your own body can be most easily learned.

Sleep
An old proverb says that he who fasts during the day will stay awake at night and should make use of the time as best he can; but, fortunately, less than 50 per cent of all fasters have any more trouble sleeping than usual. Most find that they sleep soundly and deeply, though perhaps not as long as they would otherwise.

If you find that you are not sleeping well, then here are a few tips:

Getting Ready for the Night
Switch off and wipe away the memory of the day. Do not watch exciting or provoking programmes on the television last thing at night; instead, go for a walk, read, or listen to a favourite record. In other words, do something you know will relax you. Your sleep is influenced by your waking life, so take steps not to have it disturbed.

Let your mind become a blank.

Take a stroll in the fresh air.

Take an increasingly warm foot bath followed by a cold rinse (p. 37).

Fill the bath with cold water up to the calves of your legs and wade around in it.

Do some push-ups or knee-bends to drain the blood from your head to your muscles.

Do not go to bed with cold feet.

Lack of oxygen will disturb your sleep, so turn off the heating. Sleep with your windows wide open: if you are cold, put on an extra blanket.

Do not take sleeping tablets or pain killers unless absolutely necessary. Try every natural means first.

Night
You may be troubled in the night by discomfort, stomach ache, and restlessness. Help yourself by observing the following:

A full stomach doesn't like to think, so also does it not like to sleep. Even during a fast you can feel full because of the gases in your stomach. During the night you may be particularly susceptible to cramps, and the best treatment for these is a cold compress. Take a linen towel and soak a third of it in cold water. Wring it out and fold it into three. Now put the wet side against your body, cover it with a bath towel and tie it around yourself with the cord of your pyjamas. Within no time at all it will be beautifully warm.

If you are the sort who tosses and turns and eventually has to get up and wander around, then wash yourself from head to foot in cold water — but do it with a washcloth, don't take a shower — then lie down in bed again without drying yourself. You will be surprised how well this simple method works.

Many people find that when they are fasting they sleep very lightly and not for long. If this happens to you, then take the advice of the old proverb and use your time as best you can. Do not worry that you aren't getting enough sleep — enjoy the silence of the night or the beauty of the dawn and let your thoughts wander where they will.

Think about your family or your career, and do not shy away from thinking about yourself. Take a pencil and a piece of paper and write down whatever comes into your head. Many people have found this a good time to sort out their own lives, to really find themselves and the answers to problems that have been plaguing them for a long time. Read. Everyday life often leaves so little time for reading.

When you get up the next morning you will find that you're not even tired. It is only if you don't know what to do with yourself while you are lying awake that you will start the day heavy-eyed and irritable. It is accepted that the faster needs only five or six hours of sleep, especially if he has been resting as recommended during the day.

Warmth

Don't be surprised if you find that fasting gives you cold hands and feet. The body's heating system can indeed produce heat from its food reserves, but it will have switched itself down to a minimum to economize as best it can.

Here's how you can keep yourself warm:

Dress in light but warm natural fibres, like cotton and wool, which are absorbent and retain body heat. Avoid synthetic fibres.

Wear shoes with cork or leather soles. In summer wear sandals or wooden clogs.

Exercise will warm you up.

Warm drinks will feel better than cold.

Soak your feet in a bowl of warm water.

Make a warm compress for your abdomen.

If you feel frozen right through, have a foot bath: fill the bath to your calves with lukewarm water and stand in it; then gradually add more and more hot water. In 15 to 20 minutes your body will be warm all the way through. To finish off, give your feet a quick cold rinse, then dress warmly or get into bed.

When bathing or swimming, your body will get cold more quickly than usual, so give yourself less time in the water and warm yourself up thoroughly afterwards.

What Differences Will I Notice When Fasting

Sight
You will notice that your eyes are not as sharp as usual — the words will begin to swim on the page before you. This is because the eyes tend to relax when fasting. There is nothing to worry about; they will return quickly to normal. Fasting will improve rather than impair the sight. But drivers take note: your concentration may be diminished and your reactions slowed down.

Understanding
You might find that you read a passage two or three times and still don't understand it. Your brain just can't seem to take it in. Don't let this worry you; it will correct itself in a few days.

Observation
It is quite possible that you will be more forgetful than usual and that appointments and telephone numbers will slip your mind. But is it surprising that your brain should want to take a rest too? It is merely switching off to recover from the demands made on it by everyday life.

Sexual Potency
Fasting can have very different effects on sexual potency. You might find yours diminished or increased; but, when the fast is over, you should find it has improved and become more regular.

Menstruation
The effects on this are again varied: your period could be weaker or stronger, but will become regular after the fast is over.

State of Mind
Most people feel released and relieved after a couple days of fasting because they have realized that it is doing them good. Their surprise at how good they are feeling gives them a new lease on life.

Of course it's not all a bed of roses: there are times when you will feel down, and these usually occur in the morning. Most people go through a couple of hours each day when they feel flat and tired, perhaps a bit dizzy, too. What is to be done? Should you try to buck yourself up, or just let yourself go? Both can do you good.

Whether it is just a passing mood or a general physical stagnation, the first thing to try and do is to wake yourself up. If you succeed in doing this, you will feel better both physically and mentally.

If you feel the same after you have tried a walk in the fresh air or taken part in some other activity, then it is time to let yourself wind down. Go to your room and lie down; take a book with you or just close your eyes.

But *activity* is the best cure for people who usually tend to be overweight or physically lazy. If you have too many pounds to carry around with you, you will easily lose pleasure in exercise; and, if you are just lazy, you will have let yourself go to the point where you're completely out of condition. In both cases, you need to stir yourself into activity. As your weight goes down and you start to exercise, it will get easier all the time. The day will come when you will have conquered your apathy, and exercise will be a pleasure to you. More than that, it will be a necessity. Until it is, make yourself keep going!

Low Blood-Pressure
People with very low blood-pressure (below 100/60) usually have a harder time than others. They may experience weakness, dizziness, or disturbed concentration during a fast. Their circulation needs help.

Pay particular attention to the instructions at the beginning of the chapter on getting up in the morning.

Take black tea with a teaspoonful of honey in the morning and after your nap with a warm compress. It is best to drink it while still lying down. Ginseng tea would serve as well.

Physical activity is absolutely essential but must be undertaken slowly.

Fasting Crisis
A fasting crisis seldom occur's during a short fast if you are healthy to begin with. It is more likely to crop up if you continue your fast for 20 days or more. But when problems arise, they come completely out of the blue. You may feel apathetic, irritated, or depressed, and anything that troubled you before you began your fast is likely to flare up again quite suddenly.

But, if you experience minor upsets while fasting it is just the body's way of healing itself. These are the times when the body will be expelling more poisons than ever and as soon as the waste

FASTING DIARY

Fast days	menu (see p. 24)	waste disposal (excretion)	physical condition
the day before			
1st day of fasting			
2nd day of fasting			
3rd day of fasting			
4th day of fasting			
5th day of fasting			
1st day of eating			
2nd day of eating			
3rd day of eating			

Week from......to......

mental condition (mood, dreams)	physical activity (what did you do? Exercise)	mental activity (How successful was it?)

has been eliminated, the symptoms will disappear without a trace.

On a day of illness it is obvious that the body has a lot to do and must be protected.

Lie in bed, keep warm, and, for the speediest results, give yourself an enema. Drink as much tea and water as you can. A glass of buttermilk at this point can work wonders. Avoid all exertion.

Fasting Diary and Balance Sheet
Ask yourself what new experiences fasting has brought to me? It is always rewarding to be able to answer this question, and to do so you should keep a careful check on your progress during the week. You can do this in two ways:

Diary
Keep daily notes of what you eat and what you excrete, how you feel physically and mentally and what physical and mental activity you indulge in.

Balance Sheet:
Write down everything that troubled you before your fast began, whether you think it is important or not, and after the fast is over, make a list of the problems that still persist. Draw up a balance to see what good your fast has done you.

You will find the diary and balance sheets on pages 40 and 42. A word of warning: don't expect miracles from your fast! Your balance sheet will naturally record more interesting facts after a longer fast.

BALANCE SHEET
Write down here everything that bothered you before you started fasting. After the week is over, check how many things still bother you.

Before fasting	After fasting
....	....
....	....
....	....

Before fasting	After fasting
....	....
....	....
....	....
....	....
....	....
....	....
....	....
....	....
....	....
....	....

Weight
This chart represents the fasting progress of a man and a woman who were overweight.

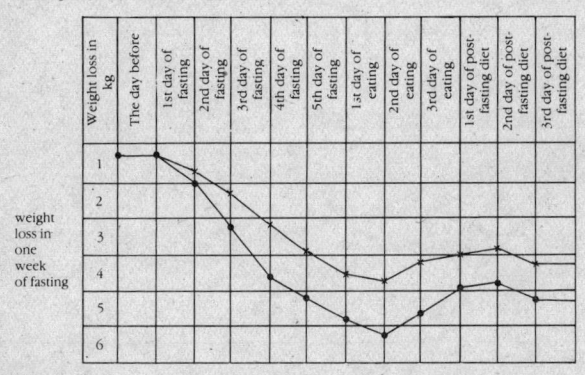

Weight loss in kg	The day before	1st day of fasting	2nd day of fasting	3rd day of fasting	4th day of fasting	5th day of fasting	1st day of eating	2nd day of eating	3rd day of eating	1st day of post-fasting diet	2nd day of post-fasting diet	3rd day of post-fasting diet
1												
2												
3												
4												
5												
6												

weight loss in one week of fasting

Example 1(x-x) woman, 40 yrs old, 5ft. 3in. tall, weight at the beginning of the fast, 143 lbs.
Example 2(o-o) man, 40 yrs old, 5ft. 8in. tall, weight at beginning of the fast, 175 lbs.

The woman's line shows a regular descent and ascent, whereas the man's drops more steeply between the first and the third days of fasting and climbs higher during the first and third days of eating. Between the fourth and fifth days the man's weight loss is negligible. This is typical for someone whose body retains a lot of salt and water, the water being used to dissolve remaining stores of salt and flush them out through the kidneys. There is no reason to become discouraged when such a standstill in weight loss occurs.

The real weight loss at the end of the week of fasting can be appreciated only on the morning of the first post-fast day diet. The woman has lost 6 pounds (2.7kg), and the man 8 pounds (3.6kg). This is the average weight loss for both over a series of fasts. The actual curve shows the loss of fatty tissues, salt, and water. The woman lost about 3 pounds (1.3kg) of fat during the week and the man 5 pounds (2.2kg). Two pounds of fat converts into 6000, calories so it can easily be seen that the woman had 1500 calories to burn up every day and the man 2100.

Let's take this further: the faster needs 30 per cent less energy because his digestive system is inactive. This means that the woman had just as much energy at her disposal (1500 calories + 30 per cent) as a woman the same age and height who was taking in 2000 calories a day.

The man had as much energy at his disposal (2100 calories + 30 per cent) as if he had been taking in 2800 calories a day. On this amount of energy you can live, participate in sports and be mentally active. Despite the fact that you are losing weight you do not lack energy, liveliness, or spirit.

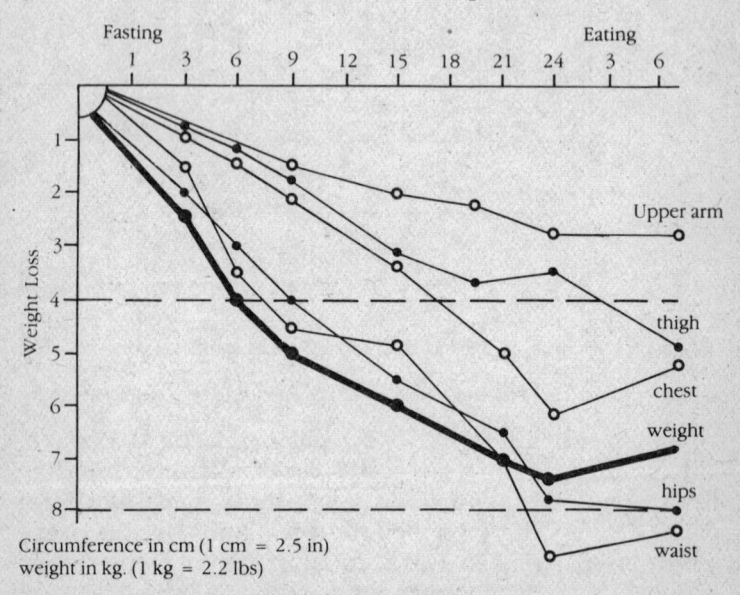

Weight loss after a fast of four weeks.
  Weight is lost from all parts of the body. The example shown here is of a 43 year old woman, 5ft tall, who weighed 143 lbs at the beginning of the fast.

Weight Charts

Keep a record of your own weight loss — you can use the tables on p. 46. The first entry you should make is what you weigh on the morning of the day before your fast. Make sure that you weigh yourself at the same time each day: always in the morning after you have passed water, but before you change out of your night clothes; or always in the morning after you have had a bowel movement and your shower, still in the nude. Jot down exactly when you weigh yourself at the top of the chart.

On the morning of your first post-fast day diet you will be able to see how much weight you have lost over the week. But don't stop there — continue to weigh yourself every day after the fast is over — it's the surest way of keeping your weight under control.

This diagram shows how effective fasting can be in helping you to change your eating habits over a long period of time: by fasting once a year for four years this man has been able to bring his weight down by about 45 pounds (20kg) which, meant that he started by being 40 per cent overweight and ended up 10 per cent overweight.

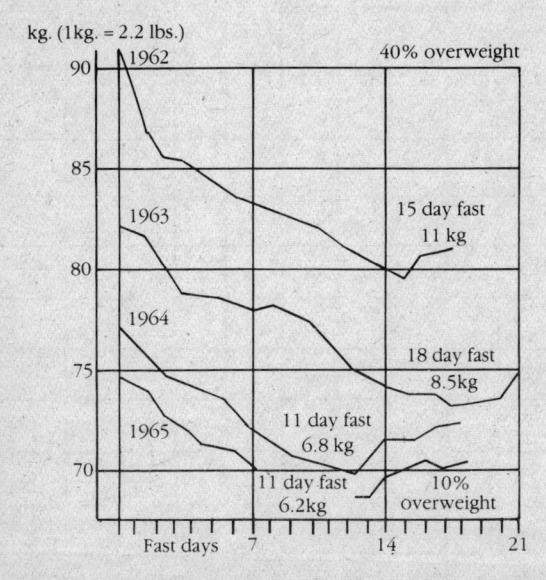

This chart shows gradual weight loss achieved after four fasts separated by periods of moderate eating. The figures were taken from a man of 43, 5ft. 9in. tall, who weighed 200 lbs. before he began his first fast.

YOUR PERSONAL WEIGHT CHART

Date	Day of the week	Weight in kg
	Morning of the day before	
	Morning of the first day of fasting	
	Morning of the 2nd day of fasting	
	Morning of the 3rd day of fasting	
	Morning of the 4th day of fasting	
	Morning of the 5th day of fasting	
	Morning of the 1st day of eating	
	Morning of the 2nd day of eating	
	Morning of the 3rd day of eating	
	Morning of the 1st day of post-fasting diet	

Weight loss in kg	The day before	1st day of fasting	2nd day of fasting	3rd day of fasting	4th day of fasting	5th day of fasting	1st day of eating	2nd day of eating	3rd day of eating	1st day of post-fasting diet	2nd day of post-fasting diet	3rd day of post-fasting diet
1												
2												
3												
4												
5												
6												
7												
8												

Weight before fasting _ _ _ _ _

Weight on morning of first post-fast day _ _ _ _ _

What have you actually lost during the week

The Losers Are the Winners
It sounds like a paradox, but it neatly sums up what I have been saying in the preceeding chapters.

The body of the faster is supplied with heat and energy from its store of fat. What is interesting is that the body does not just use fat indiscriminately. It breaks down the store in the following order: excess fat and unnecessary fat, everything that disturbs the organism, everything that makes it ill.

In a normal fasting period it does not break down: anything that is useful, any working parts of the body, anything that is necessary for life.

Behind this set of sensible rules, which the body seems to observe of its own accord, lies the secret of fasting. If you fast, this is what you gain: By the expulsion of water, salts, poisons and waste from the body, you gain well-being, and, through weight loss, you become your true self.

Too Much Protein
It is important to note that we become ill not only from eating too much fat and carbohydrates, but also from eating too much protein. This has been shown in recent studies in the field of capillary biology. Excess protein collects on the walls of tiny blood vessels (capillaries) that can be found in every internal organ. These deposits represent the preliminary stages of illness, which do not become clinically evident until many years later. This is true for all metabolic illnesses, as well as most coronary and circulatory defects which may eventually lead to a heart attack or a stroke. These protein deposits may also lead to the most common form of joint and soft tissue rheumatism and gout — to give but a few examples.

Cleansing

We can do something to avoid these dangers by ridding our bodies of excess protein deposits by fasting, and we can also learn how to cut down on these unnecessary protein deposits in the first place by proper nutrition (i.e., by reducing our protein intake). Fasting and moderation in our eating habits belong together.

Especially in the United States and in Europe we seem to be obssessed with the idea that the more protein the better. However, scientific studies show that an excess of protein clogs the walls of our cells and results in protein toxicity.

Detoxification

In this process of cleansing while on a fast, our bodies are at the same time detoxified. Toxins are deposited in the fat and protein in the body tissues. During a fast, when fat and protein are broken down, the toxins are also released and can be eliminated.

Protein While Fasting?

Now you are certain to understand why we consider it wrong to enrich fasting liquids with protein concentrates or to prescribe a regular 'protein drink'. This prevents the process of detoxification from taking place.

Of course it is a different matter in the case of extremely overweight patients on long fasts. (Those lasting more than 30 days should take place only in a clinic). The main thing for those patients is weight reduction rather than cleansing and detoxification.

I recommend that you read: *Diet and Nutrition - A Holistic Approach* by Rudolph Ballentine, M.D. published by the Himalayan International Institute; Honsdale, Pennsylvania, especially pages 111-155.

The Healthier You

Weight loss sets off a chain reaction in the body. It brings relief to the knee joints, the feet, and the vertebrae because these are the points which bear the bulk of the body's weight. It lessens the work load of the heart, which can now pump blood around the body more efficiently and strongly. Breathing becomes easier because the lungs can take in more oxygen, which reaches the cells more quickly. High blood-pressure goes down.

If your blood-pressure is too low, you may feel tired and dizzy for a while, but this will soon pass. If the sugar level of your blood

Fat content in blood

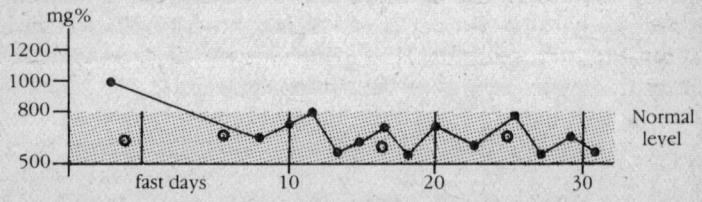

This graph shows how the fat content in the blood decreases. (It will not do so if the level is normal already.) Taken from a sample of 60 patients.

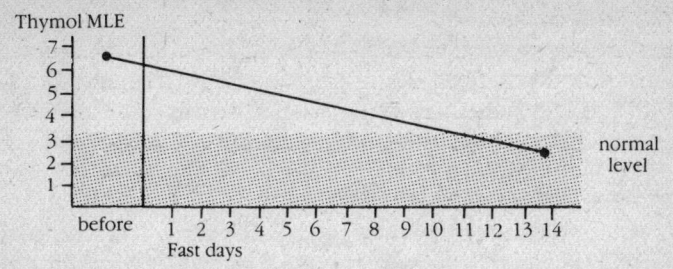

Damage to liver cells is repaired during fasting. This graph shows the results obtained from 100 patients.

is too high, it will sink to a normal level (but never below it) within the first five days of fasting. (If you are a diabetic dependent on insulin, you should fast only under medical supervision.) If your blood has too high a cholesterol content this will decrease daily. As soon as the fat level has become normal, excess fat will be broken down from all fatty internal organs, the liver, blood vessels — the body does not only lose fat that you can see.

If you have a liver complaint of any sort, laboratory tests prove that five days fasting help to put it right — provided you stay strictly away from alcohol during that time, of course. In fact, laboratory tests and private records both show that the body exercises its natural tendencies to heal itself during fasting.

There is one matter that deserves special attention: uric acid level in the urine goes up during fasting. This shows that more cells are being broken down and reconstituted than before. A few people are affected by this increase in uric acid. If you are one of them, you must strictly observe the following rules:

Make sure that you drink a lot, but avoid alcohol at all times (it is of course harmful during a fast anyway). Drink the juice of two or three lemons per day - either squeeze them beforehand or suck the juice direct from the fruit. Urinate as often as you can. If you are taking medicine prescribed by your doctor for gout or to lessen the acidity of urine, you should continue treatment during the fast. The uric acid level will drop, but only after five or six days after the fast has ended.

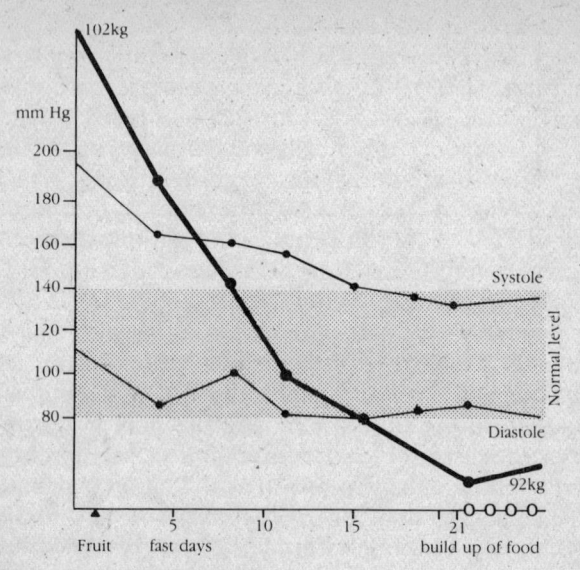

This graph shows how the blood-pressure is normalized and weight is lost after a three weeks' fast. A sample of 15 overweight people was used for this experiment.

The More Attractive You

As a doctor who has supervised many fasts, I have always been amazed by the changes in the faster's facial appearance. Here are three examples:

1. A puffy florid face with red patches (which the layman usually considers as a sign of health) will begin to relax and regain its normal shape after only five days of fasting. Cloudy eyes become clear and sparkling; a wavering gaze grows steady.

2. The brownish-grey skin of the smoker gets fresher and clearer, and the florid face of the heavy drinker with its large open pores becomes thinner, more mobile and paler. Growing self-confidence is to be read in the new, healthier features.

3. The greyish skin and worn-out look that characterizes the person who is physically and mentally exhausted also undergoes transformation. The sufferer will withdraw into himself for a while, and his face will appear thin and drawn. But then it will begin to fill out again, this time with the blood of health. His eyes will grow bright and clear.

After the faster has begun to eat again his skin will fill out and little folds and creases disappear. Impurities will have disappeared, and the skin will be smooth and clear.

How Can Your Partner Help?

Whether both partners are fasting or not it is important to realize that fasting means withdrawing into yourself and obeying the natural rhythms of your body; in other words, behaving as your body, and not your partner, tells you. The faster will be breaking all his normal habits and living by a different set of rules. You should let him go his own way, in order to find him better afterwards. Both of you should be well informed about all aspects of fasting. Decide together when the fast should begin. Make sure you agree on where you are going to hold the fast, what is actually to be consumed, how your leisure time is to be occupied, and when you are to rest.

Change your sleeping habits: because of strong body odours given off during fasting and the differing needs for fresh air, it is a good idea to sleep in separate rooms for the duration of the fast. This will enable both partners to feel free to get up or to switch on the light without disturbing each other.

Your sexual life will not necessarily be affected, but it is a possiblity you will have to reckon with. You must be ready to accept a change in your partner — it will only be temporary.

You should respect your partner's need for peace and quiet at all times.

Make sure you pay special attention to personal hygiene.

Your partner may undergo several changes of mood. Accept this without grumbling.

You must naturally do everything you can to prevent your partner being tempted by food, drink, or cigarettes.

Temptations Overcome

The faster would not be human if he was not faced with temptation at every turn. 'I'll just have a little bit!' 'Surely one apple can't hurt!' Well, an apple wouldn't do you any serious harm, but every little bit that you eat will weaken your resolve to continue the fast because it will re-awaken your appetite. If you excite your digestive juices you shouldn't be at all surprised that they demand something to digest. Experienced fasters know that it is far easier to eat nothing than it is to nibble. But you might ask yourself: 'How would it be if I just had a cup of coffee — no calories to worry about there? Or maybe some ice-cream?' Coffee and ice-cream are very tempting for the stomach, and they arouse hunger just like any other edible substance. Therefore, they should be avoided at all costs.

However, it is far more dangerous to give in completely to temptation and treat yourself to a full meal which includes, say, soup, a main course, and a dessert. This could have very serious consequences indeed, ranging from severe stomach cramps to complete collapse (see the section on Common Mistakes Made in Getting Back to Normal p. 57). It is obviously far more dangerous to break the rules while you are fasting than during your return to normal eating.

If you manage not to break your fast, your achievement will have a deeper meaning for you: every temptation overcome adds to strength of character; every weakness vanquished is another step on the road to maturity.

It is probably better not to subject yourself voluntarily to temptation in the first few days of fasting by gazing into the windows of butchers and bakers, but you will be amazed to find that it takes only a very little while to be able to do this and remain completely unaffected by the sight of food. You will be able to sit in a restaurant and drink mineral water, or maybe a glass of pure orange juice and look around you at the people eating and drinking, completely unmoved. The pride that you feel as you walk home afterwards will be totally justified. You will have proved your own strength of character.

Ask yourself how much you want a cigarette. How badly do you need to smoke and drink merely from habit or whether you are truly addicted. To give up smoking and drinking during a fast is necessary for health, but it will also tell you whether you are master of your habits, or they are master of you. Here as elsewhere you will find that a definite 'no' at the beginning of the week will help you enormously to give up altogether during the fast. If you let yourself have a puff here and a sip there you will soon find yourself in trouble.

At the end of the fast you will have gained so much confidence in yourself about your life. For example, why not continue to renounce whatever is harmful to your body? Fasting is renunciation, and this week of fasting will allow you to practise and get used to the idea of saying 'no'.

CHAPTER FOUR
BREAKING THE FAST

Shopping For the Return to Normal Eating

On the fifth day of fasting you should go out shopping. It will be a pleasure to shop again and to choose your food without feeling that you are dependent on it. This is what you will need for the first two days of your return to normal eating:

1 pound (455g) apples (organically grown if possible)
1 can tomato, potato, or asparagus soup
Butter or low-fat margarine (from health food store)
1 carton cream cheese
1 carton cottage cheese
2 yogurts
1 wholewheat bread (from your health food shop or bakery)
1 box crispbreads
1 box prunes or figs
Hazelnuts

If you are going to be cooking your main meals yourself, you also need lettuce, carrots, tomatoes, potatoes, and seasonings. If you can find food that has been organically grown, it will not only be healthier, but you will enjoy eating it more as your palate will have been refined by the fast.

If you are eating out in a restaurant, choose those items on the menu that correspond most closely with the menu further on.

The Right Way to Break Your Fast

George Bernard Shaw, who was an experienced faster, said: 'Any fool can go on a fast, but it takes a wise man to break it properly.'

Why is it so difficult? Breaking the fast means simply the building up of food intake and the corresponding increase of metabolic and digestive activity. It is usually easier for the body to get used to fasting than it is to accustom itself to eating again. The stomach has become used to the fact that it is not producing digestive juices — now it must start all over again, and it takes time. This is why it is important to treat the first days of getting back to normal as an integral part of the fast, and why you should still stick strictly to the rules. For the swiftest and easiest return to normal digestive activity, you should continue to rest as much as you did while fasting and observe these three important rules:

Eat slowly. Gulping your food can be harmful.

Chew throughly. Digestion begins in the mouth.

Don't talk while you eat. Concentrate on your food to get the most enjoyment from it.

Starting to eat again does not mean you have to go back to the bad habits you gave up with your fast. This is the time to give them up for ever and start to eat sensibly and in moderation.

THE MENU TO HELP YOU
1st day of eating
Morning: tea
Breakfast: an apple or apple sauce.
Midday: a bowl of potato and vegetable soup.
Afternoon: an apple or apple sauce.
Evening: a bowl of tomato or asparagus soup.
1 yogurt with 1 teaspoonful flaxseed, 1 crispbread.
Don't forget to put two prunes or a fig in water to soak for the next morning.

2nd day of eating
Morning: 2 prunes or a fig, 2 crispbread.
1 teaspoonful butter, 4 tablespoonsful cottage cheese with herbs.
Midday: lettuce or carrot salad (or 1 whole raw carrot — chew each mouthful thoroughly); 2 baked potatoes; light vegetables such as tomatoes, carrots, asparagus, or spinach.
For dessert: cottage cheese with 1 teaspoonful of flaxseed.
Afternoon: an apple and 10 hazelnuts.
Evening: 1 or 2 tomatoes, 1 tablespoonful butter or margarine, 1 slice wholewheat bread, cream cheese.

In the morning you can drink tea — or coffee substitute made from grains — and in the evening peppermint tea.

The third day of eating should be approached in much the same way, observing these basic rules:

Still no meat or fish must be eaten. You can have a very little of either on your fourth day. Eat raw vegetables before your meal, and remember to chew them well!

You can eat wholewheat products, plenty of fruit and vegetables, milk products, a little egg, and fats that are easily digestible, such as butter, low-fat margarine, and oils. Avoid salt and sugar.

The last third of your fasting week should be devoted to building up your food intake. This is more important than the fast itself, and your body will need rest, comfort, and time to adjust.

The Secretion of the Digestive Juices

The digestive juices are not produced during a fast, but, as you begin to eat again, they start being secreted in ever-increasing quantities, which vary from person to person.

You should not simply eat what is put before you: it is up to you to decide exactly what you can eat and how much is good for you. Do this every time you sit down to a meal.

The body that has been fasting sends out signals that you will be able to recognize more easily than before.

If your body is satisfied, you will know that you are no longer hungry and, therefore, need no more food.

If your stomach is full, it means that you have eaten more than you can digest in one go. Half-digested food causes discomfort and wind.

If your stomach refuses to take any more you will know that you have eaten far too much for your digestive system to cope with. You can stimulate your digestive juices by chewing thoroughly, eating raw fruit and vegetables, yogurt and herbs. On the other hand, you can hinder the production of the digestive juices by hurrying, worrying, getting angry, having cold feet (literally!), or eating ice-cold food.

The Circulation

About a third of the work done by the circulation is needed to keep the digestive system functioning correctly. This effort was not necessary during the fast, so do not be surprised if you are not as energetic as usual when you start to eat again. You may feel tired, light-headed or dizzy. After a meal especially, more blood is drawn to the stomach, so that the muscles and the head are deprived for a time. The solution is to lie down flat on your back after every meal; at midday take a rest in bed. Before you get up, make sure you stretch every limb and flex every muscle in your body. Do not over-exert yourself.

The 'Waterworks'
The body gets slightly dried out during fasting, and it is quite common to have a liquid intake of up to 4 quarts during the first three days of eating. You will be able to see this in the change on your bathroom scales (see also the sections on weight and weight loss). The water is necessary for the production of gastric juices and for the lubrication of the mucous membranes. It also helps to stabilize the circulation, which might take until the third day to get back to normal. Water is also needed to plump out the cells of the body and is responsible for filling out the face and smoothing the skin. To try and halt this filling-up process with artificial means like diuretics is both senseless and dangerous. You should drink as much as you want whenever you are thirsty.

The Intestines
The bowels start to function properly only when they are full — so be patient. Useful laxatives are:
    Flaxseed — take two teaspoonsful with every meal.
    Raw fruit and vegetables.
    Wholewheat bread; wholewheat flakes.
    The first normal excretion should take place on the second or third day. On no account should you use any commercial laxatives. The rectum may well be blocked with dry faeces. If you have a feeling of activity in the intestine, but sense that the rectum is blocked up, then you should use one of the following methods to clear the rectum without disturbing the rest of the intestines: a small enema with 1 pint (570ml) of water; or a glycerine suppository (available from your pharmacy).
    Normally you should have your last enema on the last day of fasting or on the first day of eating. Take only the small enema for the rectum on the third day of eating if absolutely necessary.
    After this, everything should begin to work on its own again. If you suffer from constipation here are a few tips:
    Every morning drink a glass of water on an empty stomach. If you are of a nervous disposition, drink it warm; otherwise drink it cold.
    Have soaked prunes, figs, or granola for breakfast.
    Eat food that contains plenty of roughage and chew it well. Try flaxseed, wholewheat bread, wholewheat flakes, raw fruit, and vegetables.

Get plenty of exercise.

Take your time on the toilet.

If you want regular bowels, avoid: getting up late; physical inactivity — especially after sitting at a desk all day; stress of all kinds; cold hand or feet; impatience.

What to do about wind: Place a warm damp towel on the stomach and put a hot water bottle on top of it. If you are bothered by the cold, give yourself a cold compress as described on p. 36, drink appropriate herb tea (e.g., caraway, fennel), and use a natural aid like an enema or a glycerine suppository.

Always remember that if you do not chew your food properly, you are likely to suffer from wind.

The Aftermath of Fasting

In the first few days of eating normally you may find anything that was troubling you before the fast will flare up again temporarily. No doubt this will disappoint you, but do not lose faith in the benefits of fasting. The symptoms will almost certainly disappear practically overnight, giving way to a feeling of general well-being. Only after you have completely returned to your normal life will you be able to assess the benefits of fasting for yourself. For this reason you should not be too impatient to complete your balance sheet (p. 42).

Common Mistakes in Getting Back to Normal

The high spirits which many people experience during a fast can all too often lead to overdoing it when starting to eat again. The sort of thing that can happen is best described by people who discovered it for themselves.

A group were celebrating the end of their fast in a restaurant. Mr W. had been dreaming of a nice big juicy steak the whole week, so he ordered one and devoured it greedily. Three hours later he was in bed, calling for the night nurse. 'I was suffering from the most awful stomach cramps,' he said. 'I felt I wanted to die, but couldn't.' It was only after he had vomited up the half-digested steak that the pains subsided, and he sank, white-faced and streaming with perspiration, back on to his pillow. Undigested protein in the stomach is as harmful as poison.

Mrs S. ate her way through three courses and then had an ice cream with whipped cream on top. Her bloated stomach told her she should not have done it — but worse was to follow. The next morning the scales showed that she had put on three pounds — her three-day fast had all been in vain! Every excess will show.

Mr A. was very fond of a glass of good wine and could not wait any longer. His friends had to carry him home, and medical tests showed that his liver just could not cope with the sudden soaking.

The liver needs to be protected during the first days of eating just as much as when fasting. It needs time to build up its resistance to alcohol, and just a small amount can make you drunk.

Mrs K. ate sensibly, but after the meal she ordered coffee. When she got to bed, it seemed as if the night would never end. 'I lay wide awake all night,' she said. 'Coffee never kept me from sleeping before.' The nervous system is more sensitive to coffee and other stimulants after fasting.

Mr N. ordered fish. Quite soon he knew he had had enough and he had to leave half of his meal untouched. Afterwards, he was disappointed with himself that he had not carried out his resolve to follow the recommended post-fast programme and had been persuaded to go to the restaurant with the others. The other thing that disturbed him was the fact that, during the fast, he had had such a good time without eating and drinking. Was he now to become dependent on food and alcohol for his pleasures?

The days of getting back to normal show very clearly that we depend on artificial means to heighten our spirits and improve our relationships with others.

Think again of the words of George Bernard Shaw: 'Any fool can fast, but only a wise man knows how to break a fast properly.'

Breaking the fast is the most important part of treatment. It needs time and application.

Tips For Afterwards

What is the next step? During the fast, and while you have been getting back to normal, you will have learned a lot and collected plenty of new experiences. This is the time to take the bull by the horns and change your bad eating habits once and for all.

Now that you are more confident of yourself and feel that you can actually change the direction of your life, you should put your new power to use.

Take a piece of paper and note down all the things you would like to change. You do not have to wait until after the fast is over to do this!

Draw up a plan of your food and exercise over the next few weeks. Make it suit your needs and capabilities, and do not make it so ambitious that you will give it up and go back to your old bad habits.

Keep up your ban on smoking and drinking.

Start a self-help group.

If you have fasted successfully, but still want to lose weight, then you face the question of whether to continue fasting or not. If your desire to do so is strong, and you have the facilities and the time to get back to normal gradually (always reckon with a third of your fast time for this), or you are under the supervision of a doctor, then do so by all means.

Fast for another week as soon as your business and social commitments allow you the time and opportunity. You will find that the second and third fasts are much easier than the first, but every time is different and teaches you something new. If you want to lose weight between times you can do so by fasting for very short periods at a time. Put to use your new-found discovery that you feel good and energetic without food.

Skip any meals when you have no appetite.

Fast whenever you have a fever, upset stomach, or diarrhoea — your body will thank you.

Start already to plan your next fast — maybe with friends.

Eating in Moderation

Remember what you have learned during those first few days of eating: your stomach will tell you when you have had enough. If you follow its advice you will never need a calorie chart, and the bathroom scales will bring only good news. However, most people feel happier if they know exactly what they should be eating, and there are plenty of books on healthy eating which will help you further. After a fast, all food will seem rich to you, and a little of anything will be enough. The sort of food recommended in this book — raw vegetables especially — will satisfy you quickly and not increase your weight, as they are very low in calories. But if you cannot live with a wholefood diet, then you should regularly eat only fruit, rice or raw vegetables one day a week. Try a Monday or a Friday — or both! If you are one of those people who are always hungry, then you should follow your instinct and eat five or six small meals a day. But make sure they are small and that you chew your food well. In diet books you will find many other suggestions for one-day-a-week diets — for example, they will tell you to eat only potatoes, milk, or bananas. The most important thing is that you stick to this one-day-a-week holiday for your stomach.

Giving Up Smoking and Drinking
Have you wanted to give up smoking for ages? And did you notice that fasting helped you more than anything else? Your taste buds are refreshed during fasting, and afterwards cigarettes will taste different — stale, like straw, and quite unpleasant. After you have given up smoking for a week during your fast, you will know that you can do it because you have already started. There are books available that will help you further.

You have proved to yourself during the week of fasting that you can do without alcohol. This pause in drinking was good for your liver and self-confidence. If you drink habitually, no matter what sort of alcohol you prefer, you are always in danger of becoming dependent on drink. After a week of abstinence you should be strong enough to give up drink regularly and often, if not altogether. If the week of fasting has shown you that you are somewhat dependent on drink, then do not hesitate to contact Alcoholics Anonymous — a group of experienced people whose aim is to help one another. Fasting will give you a new incentive to conquer other weaknesses.

Self-help Groups
Whether your problem is eating, drinking, smoking or whatever, it will be easier to face with a group of like-minded people than alone. If your problem is over-eating, then you should join an organization such as Weight Watchers, who encourage one another to diet with considerable success and have a lot of fun in the process. Fasters should invite fellow fasters to share their experiences — the conversation will broaden from there and you will find yourself sharing other problems, you will encourage others to do the same, and you will soon find that you are not alone.

Fasting — a Time to Think
The experience of fasting can help you reach deeper knowledge of human nature, for it is very much a time for reflection and thought. Apart from the new physical experiences of how your

body works, you will learn a lot about your inner self too. The experiences to be gained on this level are as different as the fasters themselves. From your first contact with fasting you will realize that it is a way to inner freedom and independence of thought and action. It would go beyond the bounds of this book to explain in further detail, and in any case the deeper meanings of fasting and more beneficial and permanent improvements to the health can be experienced only by the individual in a prolonged fast. The purpose of the present book will have been more than fulfilled should you be successful in long-term fasting, and I can only hope that you will have the opportunity to try it.

CHAPTER FIVE
FASTING IN A CLINIC

Everyone should fast at least once in his life. For every healthy person over forty, I recommend a general overhaul, which includes an exercise training programme and a prolonged fast. If you are overweight, a fast will help you not only to shed extra pounds, but to learn to correct your bad eating habits and so keep you slim and healthy. If your metabolism is not working properly because of an imbalanced diet or for any other reason, you should fast until medically pronounced fit. This applies if you suffer from any of the following: tendency to high blood-pressure; high fat content in the blood (cholesterol and triglycerides); high sugar content in the blood (symptom of diabetes); too many blood cells; or excess uric acid in blood (for example, in gout sufferers). In short, anyone who wants to be fit should fast. Fasting is a sensible precaution against cancer (for example, the hereditary type) or against premature ageing.

Why Should Some People Fast in a Clinic?
If you suffer from one of the diseases listed below you should not attempt to fast at home. Many sick people suffer from more than one illness, and, if you are one of these you obviously should seek medical advice. However, fasting is especially recommended for diseases connected with diet and lack of exercise.

You should fast, only in a specialized clinic, if you suffer from: dangerous overweight (more than 30 per cent); diabetes; too many blood cells; a fatty liver; chronic hepatitis (damage to the cells of the liver); gout; faulty blood supply to the heart, limbs and brain; rheumatism or arthritis; chronic skin diseases (eczema, scurf); faulty blood supply; or allergies of the skin and mucous membranes.

Many diseases that are pronounced incurable can be helped to some degree by fasting, or at least halted in their natural progress — migraine, headaches, for example.

Who Should Avoid Fasting Altogether?
People who should not fast at all are: those with no natural reserves, such as sufferers from malnutrition or severe mental or physical exhaustion (after a long illness or an operation); people suffering from an illness that is accompanied by weight loss, such as tuberculosis or cancer, the mentally ill who are unable to be responsible for themselves; the spiritually disturbed who lack inner peace.

Anyone who is under severe mental or physical stress should take a week's holiday before embarking on a long fast.

What Happens When You Fast in a Clinic?
If you go on a fasting cure in a clinic you will live with other fasters for three, four, or more weeks under the supervision of a medical team. The whole atmosphere of the clinic will be geared to fasting, and you will have to abide by a set of house rules, which will include a ban on alcohol and cigarettes and guarantee you time for a complete rest at midday and at night. Though the rules are very strict and necessarily limit your lifestyle, the fasting clinic has nothing of the institutional atmosphere of a hospital and you will be surrounded by colour, light, and comfort.

A certain way of life has emerged in German fasting clinics as the result of long experience. Great importance is laid on the post-fasting diet, as well as on exercise, such as walking, swimming, and gymnastics. The clinics are usually situated in beautiful surroundings in the countryside and encourage contact with nature — water and fresh air. There are facilities available for sauna and massage, classes in breath control and movement, lectures on health, and a cultural programme which includes music and discussion groups.

If you are beginning an extended fast in a clinic you will be reassured by the presence of experienced fasters - the doctors and nurses and fellow fasters, all of whom will be able to help you. Apart from the staff, who are on call day or night, you will have the benefit of the latest technological equipment to check and record your progress throughout your stay.

INDEX

alcohol, 49, 52, 58, 60
Alcoholics Anonymous, 60
Aly, Otto Karl, 10
appetite, 29, 51

balance sheet, 42
Ballentine, Dr Rudolph, 48
Bircher, Dr Ralph, 14
blood-pressure, high, 48
  low, 39, 48
body odour, 51
bowel movement, 25
broth-porridge fasting, 16, 27
Buchinger fasting 'clinic', 16

Carrot Broth, 27
Celery Broth, 27
cigarettes, 32, 52, 60
circulation, 20, 30, 55
cleansing, internal, 16
compress, cold, 36
constipation, remedies for, 56
contraceptive, oral, 26
cramps, stomach, 26, 52

depression, 18
diabetes, 49
diary, fasting, 40-42
Diet and Nutrition — A Holistic Approach, 48
digestive juices, 51, 55
disease, prevention and cure of, by fasting, 17
diuretics, 31, 56

enema, 26, 31, 56
energy, 33-35
Epsom salt, 24, 25, 29, 31
exercise, 30, 33, 34, 39

eyesight, 38

facial appearance, changes in, when fasting, 50
fast breaking, 53
  mistakes in, 57-58
fasting
  and energy, 10
  and feasting, 11
  and illness, 9
  basic rules for, 15
  crisis during, 39
  in a clinic, reasons for, 62
  in animals, 13
  on vacation, 20
  preparation for, 21-22
  reasons for avoidance, 63
fat, 47, 49
Flaxseed Porridge, 28
foot bath, 37

Glauber Salt, 22, 25, 26

healing fast, 17
hunger, 12
Hunzas, The, 14

laxatives, 56
liver complaints, 49
lungs, 32

menstruation, while fasting, 38
mouth, cleansing of, 33
mucous membranes, cleansing of, 32

Oat Porridge, 28
observation and understanding, 38

Potato Broth, 27
protein, 47-48, 57
psychological preparation for fasting, 23
purification, 16

rejuvenation, 17
relaxation, 35
religious fasting, 14
Rice Porridge, 28

self-help groups, 60
sexual potency, 38
Shaw, George Bernard, 58
skin, cleansing of, 17, 32
sleep, preparation for, 36
solitary fasting, 19
spiritual fasting, 33

tea fasting, 16
tea-broth-juice fasting, 16
temptation, resisting, while fasting, 51, 52
Tomato Broth, 27

uric acid, increase of when fasting, 49
urine, 31, 49

vagina, 32

water fasting, 16
water, importance of drinking, while fasting, 56
weight loss, 16, 43, 44, 45, 46
  effects of, 48
Weight Watchers, 60
workday fasting, 20
  rules for, 21